I'm Having a Ball!

Recipes with Testicles

Keith Pepperell

DEDICATION

To my spawn Jack, Lydia, and Alex none
of whom are fans

ACKNOWLEDGMENTS

Lady Estima Davenport

Muriel Dinwiddy

The Great Malcolm Hardee - The Best
Balls in the Business

Testicle Scholars Everywhere

1. BALLS WITHOUT THE CHAINS

Testicles are indeed quite funny, and eating them is not for the squeamish. Once, in a Spanish restaurant a fellow ordered the daily special Testículos de Matador con arroz. He asked the waiter what kind of testicles they were and was quietly advised, "Sometimes the bull wins."

There is all manner of folklore about the eating of bull's testicles (see *post*)

It is certainly the case that there

are a number of festivals celebrating testicle and testicle eating one of which is the much fabled Serbian event. According to Russian intelligence sources, "Every year in September the villages of Ozrem and Lunjevica in the municipality of Milanovac, Serbia, hosts the **World Testicle Cooking Championship**. The festival serves up a variety of testicles, including wildlife."

 Part of the official website translates out of the Serbian by Google as follows, "The Festival is one of the big budget. Visit us a threat big festivals. Razočaraćemo if you think here you can buy weird stuff that is imposed by the street vendors, spin on the Ringišpilu with a bottle of beer in hand, make his way through the crowd ROAR under šatrama, to hear the first voice of the Government, to leave a child in a Tin. If it's on your mind, you better don't even try to get. If you are in need of rest, nature, good companionship, good quality music and inoffensive people who entertain known and unknown, then you've come to the right place. Competitors like to operate in secrecy, without interruption, without harassment, but are always ready to take you under my roof and serve from the heart."

There are numerous other testicle festivals in the United States. There aims, claims, and publicity is most engaging. Some of which is set out *post*.

The Montana State Society Rocky Mountain Oyster Festival or "Testy Fest, "is an annual event that includes all-you-can-eat Rocky Mountain Oysters, beer, Crown Royal, and music. As one attendee Chef McGraw noted about the cattlemen who often castrated calves to control their growth and behavior, "The idea for the dish probably originated with old-time ranchers. They didn't want to waste anything,"

 McGraw, who is a Montana native, claimed he usually coated the main ingredients in flour and seasoning before deep-frying them. He serves them with a side of cocktail, ranch, or barbeque sauce, "They kind of have their own little taste," he said.

 The noted **Turkey Byron Illinois Turkey Testicle Festival** advises, "Based around Live Music acts and Deep Fried Turkey Testicles, the event is much more than that with vendors, live music, food, beverages, auctions, giveaways and much, much more. Traditionally it is a day for bikers and families to show their support in the community and throw a party for a charitable cause." Ah! One might have suspected such would be popular among the biker community.

The Deerfield, Michigan Testicle Festival is happy to claim, "This annual festival brings thousands of people to the Deerfield Legion where they can enjoy scrumptious Rocky Mountain Oysters and Bull Nuts and a nice cold beverage. It may sound odd but don't judge a book by its cover. People from other states charter buses to attend."

Some years ago, it seems, things got a bit out of hand in the **Fargo-Moorhead** area of South Dakota in anticipation of the Testicle Festival there including a three-day, 33-band rock concert. It was reported: "The chaos, at times involving at least 200 young adults and 40 officers from Fargo and other law enforcement agencies at the park, resulted in seven arrests, including one for assault on a police officer."

The Tumbleweed Calf Fry held in attractive Stillwater, Oklahoma had been increasing in popularity over its twenty-five year history and now attracts over 30,000 fans. Like other testicle festivals this includes music, goat roping, trash can basketball, and mechanical bull riding. One fan wrote, "Then there is the ever present pretty young girls dressed in short bouncy skirts and cowboy boots or extremely short cut-offs and cowboy boots. Red dirt music draws the crowds. The calf testicle must be thinly filleted to create the correct thinness and to cook properly after it has been dipped into an egg batter and coated in flour."

The Oleon, Missouri Testicle Festival Is an equally popular venue where turkey testicles are the stars. Their publicity states, "The Testicle Festival is a huge day long cook-off of deep fried turkey testicles, booths, dancing and carnivals. Located in the heart of Olean Missouri, this festival draws thousands of locals and visitors."

In Clinton, Montana **The Clinton Testicle Festival** or "Testy Festy" is described as, "A popular stop for those headed to the annual motorcycle rally in Sturgis, South Dakota. Not for the faint of stomach." Again, we

see bikers and testicle festivals go
ball in hand.

 Testy Festy is not for the faint-
hearted it seems. It was claimed "It
was attended by over 15,000 people
this year, according to a story in the
Missoulian last week. Over 5,000
pounds of Rocky Mountain Oysters were
consumed by sometimes intoxicated
attendees in various states of
undress." Another fan wrote, "During
my college years at the University of
Montana I attended the notorious
Testicle Festival on several
occasions. The festival is an annual
event (usually held for a whole
weekend in September or October) that
takes place at the Rock Creek Lodge.
At the festival, people of all ages
gather to party and consume "Rocky
Mountain Oysters" (bull testicles
beer-battered and deep fried). Don't

pass judgment either - it sounds as weird to most Montanans (myself included) as it probably sounds to the rest of you. Being a strict vegetarian, I have never actually tried one of these "tasty" treats, but I hear they taste like chicken (if you can believe that).

Regardless, the festival is a lot of fun & I highly recommend it to those who can stomach it! Oh, and I recently heard that there is also now a "Pussy Festival" held sometime in the spring; apparently they serve bobcat or mountain lion meat." No comment.

The Tiro, Ohio Testicle Festival in rural Crawford County was started by the Tiro Tavern and drew bikers and testicle lovers with its slogan: "You'll have a Ball." It is claimed 600 pounds of battered and fried calve

and pig testicles are sold annually."
Ah! bikers again.

 In the heart of cattle country the
Lemhi County Cattlewomen host the
annual **Salmon River, Idaho Testicle
Festival.** It is reported, "The family
friendly event offers home grown and
home fried rocky mountain oysters,
finger steaks and homemade side dishes
and desserts made by local
cattlewomen. The event includes a live
band and is held right out in the
field with a great portable dance
floor and plenty of room to get boot
scootin'."

Concerning **The Oakdale, California
Testicle Festival,** it is suggested,
"It is much like a Spaghetti Feed. But
our main course is…well, bull
testicles. Yep, our way of celebrating

our rich western heritage and over 30 years of cowboy traditions."

In Huntley, Illinois the Parkside Pub hosts the annual **Huntley Turkey Testicle Festival** in Huntley, Illinois - admission: $10 (testicles sold separately). The Pub's owners write, "What started years ago as joke has burgeoned into a Huntley day-before-Thanksgiving tradition. The Turkey Testicle Festival enters its 29th season of serving up batter-fried turkey testicles. Last year, it drew a festival record-breaking 4,200 guests. We expect to serve 1,000 pounds of turkey testicles this year."

However, some enterprising fellows in nearby East Dundee decided to play host to the inaugural **East Dundee Turkey Testicle Festival**. It was reported locally, "At East Dundee's

board meeting Monday, former Gilberts
Village Trustee Cliff Surges, and one
person involved with bringing the
event to East Dundee, gave a
presentation on the festival.

"(Village Administrator) Bob (Skurla)
and Karen (Blair) and your entire
marketing team have done a fabulous
job with everything going on downtown
here but we found a little chink in
the armor in November," Surges said.

He said the Turkey Testicle Festival
will include live music, food, drinks,
and, fittingly, servings of turkey
testicles.

"I think this would bring up a big
objection from the turkey community,"
joked Trustee Jeff Lynam.

"Are you representing them this
evening?" Village President Lael

Miller joked back.

Skurla said when approached about East Dundee hosting the event he was initially hesitant, "The first question out of my mouth was I wanted to know if I was going to get an angry call from Huntley," he said.

For more than 30 years, Huntley has hosted the event which draws thousands of guests to the village.

But Skurla said Huntley officials told him the event is privately sponsored.

"So it's not a case where I'm stealing someone's thunder," he said.

Surges said he envisions East Dundee's Turkey Testicle Festival presenting an opportunity to work with Elgin Community College's culinary students to come up with some testicle recipes.

East Dundee officials would only be responsible for putting up the perimeter for the event and providing security, Skurla said.

"So it's not a lot they're asking on our end," he said. "And it could be something that puts East Dundee on the map."

Perhaps even a testicle festival war will break out at some time in the future at that environs?

It seems that testicle festivals attract bikers, cowboys, girls in short cut-offs, alcoholism, and occasional fisticuffs. My kind of festivals.

2. THE WORLD OF TESTICLES

Testicle eating and testicle festivals are quite well-reported but is the attraction merely because testicles are just plain funny? In her excellent article *Cooking with Balls at the Testicle Festival* writer Kim Hartman in *Food* in the *Digital Journal* does an excellent job of introducing her reader to the mysterious world of testicle eating. She quotes a person from the Serbian Testicle Festival, "Some men would grimace at the idea of eating the testicles of an animal, but in many cultures they are considered a delicacy, an aphrodisiac and festivals are created to celebrate, prepare and feast on the coveted meat known as the testes."

She adds, "Depending on where you live, eating balls may not be that uncommon. You can find them on menus in regions big on cattle ranching

including Texas and in farming areas
throughout North America. They can be
purchased in big city specialty
markets where people from foreign
countries live, work, eat and shop. In
the United States they call them Rocky
Mountain Oysters or Mountain Oysters,
Prairie Oysters, Hog Balls, Calf Fries
and Turkey Testicles. They cook and
serve them battered, breaded, deep
fried and pan fried, as appetizers and
main course dishes as well as sliced
and fried and made into a sandwich and
enjoyed with a number of toppings
similar to a po' boy.

They can originate from beef cattle,
pigs, sheep, turkeys and ducks and
considering how much beef and pork is
consumed in North America, half of
these creatures being male, there are
plenty of mountain oysters to go
around."

Certainly, the claimed connection to both virility and aphrodisiac qualities has a long folk lore tradition. Here are some amusing anecdotes.

Dario Maestripieri a Professor of Comparative Human Development, Neurobiology, and Evolutionary Biology at the University of Chicago advises the word testify comes from the Latin word for 'testicle'. He writes in Psychology Today, "In ancient Rome, two men taking an oath of allegiance held each other's testicles, and men held their own testicles as a sign of truthfulness while bearing witness in a public forum. The Romans found a word to describe this practice but didn't invent the practice itself. Other primates had already been doing this for millions of years. Two male baboons who co-operate with each other by forming aggressive alliances against other baboons frequently fondle each other's genitalia".

In Japanese folklore the The Japanese Racoon Dog or tanuki is often depicted comically since it has a spectacularly large scrotum. It has been well put, "The comical image of the *tanuki* having a large scrotum is thought to have developed when goldsmiths would use the pelts of tanuki for the process of hammering gold nuggets into leaf. Due to the actual wild *tanuki* having disproportionately large testicles, a feature that has inspired humorous exaggeration in artistic depictions, and how gold nuggets share a homophone with testicles in the Japanese language, such associations would come to memetically link them together into its folklore image tradition of being a creature of wealth and whimsy. *Tanuki* may be shown with their testicles flung over their backs like travelers' packs, or using them as drums."

"Rocky Mountain oysters, prairie oysters, calf fries, huevos del toros (which is literally "bulls' eggs" in Spanish), cowboy caviar, Montana tendergroins, and swinging beef testicles have been consumed by ranchers for centuries." "It seems to me they have a long history," says Dr. James Hoy,"Many cultures, hunter and gatherer cultures, would not want to waste anything." He adds, "Testicles are rumored to be "aids to sexual performance by men, coming from eating the bull, the head of the herd." He concluded, "I know many ranches that will collect them during branding and when they are all done, they will then have a party. The oysters will be the main meal — a full course to go along with the beer and whiskey."

Occasionally folklore has it that some creatures have a fondness for human testicles as is the case with the Pacu Fish. This naughty relation of the piranha has been claimed to attack humans, particularly the testicles. Dr. William Fink Curator of Fishes (what a delightful job) at The University of Michigan points out that Pacus are vegetarians and there is no actual record of their ever attacking a person. The red bellied fish do have an extraordinarily terrifying set of teeth that Fink points out are used for crushing nuts (non-human) that area vital part of their diet. He informs, "Unlike piranhas, which have rigid, razor-sharp interlocking teeth, pacus have teeth that resemble human molars and fit together in a similar bite, Fink said. The pacus use those teeth to crush their food, not to rip it apart - or off."

The fun loving Scandinavians have enjoyed a ruse about testicle eating fish in the Strait of Oresund where swimmers were advised to always wear trunks. The Huffington Post took the bait (as it were) and reported, "Wear your trunks — no ifs, ands or nuts":

Further it has been humorously stated, "World cuisine is balls-deep in testicles. Male animals raised for meat are often castrated before they start getting too manly with their balls. Which means wherever there's a bull there's a ball. Start by pinning down how big you'd like your balls and the world will feed you your fill. Like them small and dainty? Head over

to Taipei where you can eat rooster
testicles, in their little scrotums,
either steamed plain or fried-up spicy
to cover up the funk. Into something
midsize between the thighs? The Middle
East grills up some nasty lamb
testicle kebabs that fit the bill. Big
and bulbous? Spain's your spot with
their bull ball bounty."

 The term 'balls' is often used to
denote bravado, courage; GUTS. In this
sense, "balls" still means
"testicles," but "having balls"
implies bravado. Having large "balls"
or many "balls" implies even more
bravado. (The "having testicles" =
"bravado" relationship exists in other
languages, e.g. "tener cojones" in
Spanish.) Further examples might
include; You've got balls to do
something like that! That fellow must

have enormous balls to climb that cliff! Or, You've got a lot of balls showing your face in this bar again.

3. INTERESTING TESTICLE FACTS AND DISPUTES

1. Scholars Troy W. Martin and Mark Goodacre (sic) had a most interesting academic squabble that Martin describes in *Project Muse* when he writes, "In 2004, I published an article in the *Journal of Biblical Literature* in which I argued that περιβόλαιον in 1 Cor 11:15 means "testicle." In the same journal in 2011, Mark Goodacre wrote a critique challenging and contesting my translation not only in this passage but also in Euripides' *Herc. fur.* 1269. In this article, I respond to Goodacre's critique and offer additional arguments supporting the translation of περιβόλαιον as "testicle" in both passages. I rely on modern linguistic theory to demonstrate that context requires the meaning of "testicle" for περιβόλαιον in both 1 Cor 11:15 and *Herc. fur.* 1269. I conclude that my reading of περιβόλαιον as "testicle" makes better sense of the use of this term in both passages than any other proposed readings, including Goodacre's."

Much more fun than a mere potato fight!

2. Polyorchidism is the unusual incidence of more than two testicles. It is a very rare conjenital disorder with fewer than 200 cases reported in medical literature and 6 cases (two horses, two dogs and two cats) in veterinary literature. A man who has polyorchidism is known as a polyorchid. The author thinks a most marvelous form of address to a chum might be, "There you are my dear old polyorchid!"

3. That highly talented and brilliantly funny writer Liam Drew, investigates in that most excellent publication *Slate* the age old question; Why are testicles kept in a vulnerable dangling sac? He reports, "Soccer fans call it *brave goalkeeping*, the act of springing into a star shape in front of an attacker who is about to kick the ball as hard as possible toward the goal. As I shuffled from the field, bent forward, eyes watering, waiting for the excruciating whack of pain in my crotch to metamorphose into a gut-wrenching ache, I thought only *stupid goalkeeping*. But after the fourth customary slap on the back from a teammate chortling, "Hope you never wanted kids, pal," I thought only *stupid, stupid testicles*. Natural selection has sculpted the mammalian forelimb into horses' front legs, dolphins' fins, bats' wings, and my soccer ball-catching hands. Why, on the path from the primordial soup to us curious hairless apes, did evolution house the essential male reproductive organs in an exposed sac? It's like a bank deciding against a vault and keeping its money in a tent on the sidewalk. It's rather humbling to realize that this basic aspect of our bodies remains a mystery. The fact that such a ridiculous appendage evolved twice surely means we should be able to get a handle on it. A successful theory will have to explain the full diversity of mammalian testicle positions, not just the scrotum's existence. I like Chance and Frey's galloping hypothesis, but could a scrotum really be the only way to deal with undulating abdominal pressure? In addition, do scrotal sperm really differ fundamentally from internally generated tiddlers? Can we definitively prove temperature sensitivity evolved after the expulsion of the scrotum? And signaling is still an outside bet, but if scrotums were really sexually selected, where's the mammalian peacock, some species toting a pair of soccer balls? Talking of which, while we wait for a final answer, the *scrotality totality, us soccer goalkeepers should probably look to our baseball-playing friends who use evolution's gift of a large brain and* opposable thumbs to don a protective cup."

4. Aristotle was a bit of a bugger
and he was often right but sometimes
wrong. He notes that if you "mutilate"
a boy — lop off his testicles — his
voice never breaks and he never grows
bald: he becomes feminized. The
inference that women are **naturally
mutilated men** is not entirely
unreasonable, although try getting
away with that at a Quilting B and get
away with both in one piece!

5. However, in Aristotle's *History of
Animals* (350 BC) he plays considerable
attention to testicles and their
location. Broadly, he considers the
natural location of testicles is
"between the legs" so it would follow
legless creatures (excluding drunks)
most likely do not have testicles. He
writes "Of male animals the genitals
of some are external, as is the case

with man, the horse, and most other creatures; some are internal, as with the dolphin. With those that have the organ externally placed, the organ in some cases is situated in front, as in the cases already mentioned, and of these some have the organ detached, both penis and testicles, as man; others have penis and testicles closely attached to the belly, some more closely, some less; for this organ is not detached in the wild boar nor in the horse."

And further, "The penis of the elephant resembles that of the horse; compared with the size of the animal it is disproportionately small; the testicles are not visible, but are concealed inside in the vicinity of the kidneys; and for this reason the male speedily gives over in the act of intercourse.

Again, "The serpent genus is
similar and in almost all respects
furnished similarly to the saurians
among land animals, if one could
only imagine these saurians to be
increased in length and to be
devoid of legs. That is to say, the
serpent is coated with tessellated
scutes, and resembles the saurian
in its back and belly; only, by the
way, it has no testicles. No fish
has a neck, or any limb, or
testicles at all."

Again, "Oviparous blooded quadrupeds
are unprovided with ears, but possess
only the passage for hearing; neither
have they breasts, nor a copulatory
organ, nor external testicles, but
internal ones only; neither are they
hair coated, but are in all cases

covered with scaly plates. Moreover, they are without exception saw-toothed."

In the modern era, Whalerock Media provides us with similar accounts.

"While some reptiles become male because of their genes, others initiate testicular development as a response to incubation temperatures. Pollution can cause some reptiles to exhibit hormonal imbalances that lead to the feminization of males or the masculinization of females. The male reptiles, like all other vertebrates, have paired gonads that produce sperm and testosterone. Reptiles carry their testicles or testes internally, often in close proximity to the kidneys. Testicles are sex organs, or gonads, whose primary job is to produce and store sperm. Unlike human testicles, which produce sperm on a relatively consistent basis, many reptiles' only do so while undergoing a seasonal testicular enlargement that coincides with the breeding season. Testicles also function as endocrine glands, producing testosterone. This is important for the development of secondary sexual characteristics, such as the dewlaps, crests and flamboyant plumage characteristic of many male reptiles."

The author knows of several men who sport unusually flamboyant plumage, although he is unable to attest whether or not they are truly reptilian - save a well-known, and quite obvious political figure.

5. TESTICLE RECIPES

Chef Ljubomir Erovic, who wrote the

first ever gonad cookbook, *The Testicle Cookbook – Cooking with Balls* claims testicles are rich in testosterone and are believed to be a powerful aphrodisiac in China as well as his homeland of Serbia. He includes recipes form stallions, ostriches, bulls, pigs and turkeys.

He claims sheep and stallion testicles have the most aphrodisiac properties.

Erovic also organizes the Serbian based World Testicle Cooking Championship drawing chefs from Australia, Bosnia-Herzegovina, Finland, Greece, Hungary, Norway and of course Serbia.

Whether they are an aphrodisiac, as Erovic claims is unclear, but here are some of my favorite recipes made from commonly available product.

Testicle preparation is a little tricky but one noted chef suggests the following, "Testicles have two membranes that surround the glands.

 The outer membrane encases the balls — a sack, if you will. Kitchen sheers help to cut through the tough tissue which can then be peeled back and torn away from the inner membrane.

 This inner membrane (*tunica albuginea*, for those of you following along in your copy of *Gray's Anatomy*) is what makes the balls explode when they are heated. It can shrink rapidly when it comes in contact with heat, forcing its contents (the actual gland) to shoot all over the inside of your oven.

To avoid this (and you want to avoid this), the inner membrane needs to be punctured, allowing it to shrink away from the testicle."

1. Auntie Rotter's Rocky Mountain Oysters Recipe

Auntie Rotter is an elderly former biker's moll who is legendary in the Dakotas for her skills with a machete, her ability to drink a table under itself, and her testicle recipes. Now a plucky ninety-three-year-old Auntie Rotter has attended Sturgis annually for all seventy-seven years of their holding the event. She still arm wrestles, drinks Pabst, and is regularly tattooed.

Ingredients

2 pounds walnut sized calf testicles (not bull's)
2 cups Pabst Blue Ribbon beer
2 nice large fresh brown eggs, beaten

1 1/2 cups all-purpose flour

1/4 cup best yellow cornmeal

Nun-blessed salt and ground white
pepper to taste

Enough best cooking oil to cover your
testicles while frying

1 tablespoon of your favorite hot
pepper sauce

Method

With a very sharp knife, very
carefully split the tough, nasty
tasting outer skin-like muscle that
surrounds each calf's testicle and
remove it.

Slice each calf's testicle into
approximately half inch thick ovals or
you can cook them whole if they are
small.

Put slices in a bowl and cover them
with Pabst. Leave them to comfortably

linger there for a couple of hours.

Drink three Pabst Beers and think about getting a new tattoo on your testicles.

Forget the former.

In another bowl, combine the nice fresh brown eggs, all-purpose flour, cornmeal, salt, and white pepper.

Remove slightly sozzled testicles from beer and dredge.

Heat oil to 375 F and deep fry for three minutes or so. They should turn a lovely golden-brown color.

Drain on paper towels and serve nice and hot with your favorite hot sauce and three more beers.

Think about a fight.

2. Minnesota Slim's Turkey Nuts

Minnesota Slim was a well-known alcoholic, 'shine maker, turkey rustler, and card cheat. He finally met his match at the hands of Dead-Eye Jean-Luc 'Pinky' Dubonnet following a disagreement over what should accompany a turkey nut dish - should it be baguette or sourdough.

In the legendary **Bun Fight at the OK Corral** 'Slim' was shot in the testicles by Pinky Dubonnet and his famous recipe was splattered all over a sidewalk.

Ingredients

3 pounds of fresh turkey nuts (located near the Turkey's liver)
1 pound of all-purpose flour
Nun-blessed salt and ground white pepper (to season flour)

Your favorite hot sauce

Method

Season your all-purpose flour to taste

Heat your oil in a deepish fryer to 350-degrees.

Rinse your nuts under cold running water and pat them very dry with a paper towel.

Make a lengthwise slit with a very sharp knife along your nuts to butterfly them. Don't cut them in half.

Dredge in the seasoned flour removing any excess and fry them immediately. About three minutes until golden brown will suffice

Have a platter with a fresh paper

towel ready to drain your nuts.

Immediately serve your nuts with your choice of sauce.

Drink some moonshine and consider putting together a poker game.

3. Granny Johnson's Church Social Pickled Hog's Testicles

Blessed among Grannies, Muriel 'Knuckles' Johnson has been a vital force in every aspect of senior affairs in her community, including her well-attended workshops "Foreplay Conversations" and "Getting a Handle on Ladies Toys".

The dear lady's parting shot of "Happy Hoggin'!" is legendary in that part of the Mid-West green bean casserole belt. She avows, "There is nothing better to get the ball rolling at a Church Cook-Out than a nice bucket of pickled hog nuts."

Ingredients

12 big fat juicy hog's testicles

1 1/2 cups of white vinegar
(distilled)
1 ½ cups fresh water
1 tablespoon favorite pickling spice
1 crushed clove of garlic
1 fresh bay leaf

Directions

Cover hog's testicles with water in a
saucepan and bring to a nice rolling
boil and then turn off heat and let
the testicles steep in the water for
about eleven minutes or so

Mix some the other ingredients
(vinegar, water, and pickling spice)
together in another saucepan over a

medium heat and bring to a rolling
boil. Add the crushed garlic and bay
leaf. Remove from the heat and then
fill your Ball Jars (sic) or Mason
Jars with the testicles mixed in with
the hot white vinegar. Keep in a
refrigerator for ten days or so. Serve
at a church Social or Church Picnic.

4. Cletus 'Rodent Man' Habsfield's Squirrel Oysters

Squirrels are annoying tree rats but
are considered a country delicacy by
turnip-eater Cletus and his gun toting
chums. Squirrels are small or medium-
size rodents and have a frightful
array of relatives including tree
squirrels, marmots, woodchucks, flying
squirrels, woodchucks, and prairie
dogs. Squirrels breed thirty times a
year and give birth to a varying

number of young (250-700) after three to six weeks, depending on species. The young are born naked, toothless, and blind. They become sexually mature at the end of the first day. Squirrels enjoy eating snakes, chickens, swans, whales, sharks, and wildebeest.

Packs of squirrels have been known to both attack and devour human beings, particularly on camp grounds and in trailer parks.

There are approximately seventy-five trillion squirrels in the United States. All species of squirrels have particularly tasty testicles.

Rodent Operative Cletus Habsfield hunts squirrels with hand and stick grenades, machine and Gatling guns, sticks of dynamite, and most conveniently with his ancient Camino.

Ingredients

1 lb. of squirrel testicles

1 cup all-purpose flour

Nun-blessed salt and ground white pepper to taste

1 teaspoon favorite smoked paprika

1 quart favorite vegetable oil

Method

Season the squirrel testicles with salt, pepper, and a good pinch of smoked paprika. Drink a beer

Roll the testicles in flour- shake off any excess

Add 1/2 to 3/4 inch vegetable oil to a large skillet.

Heat to approximately 375 degrees F

Carefully place squirrel pieces in hot oil (do not overlap them or overfill the skillet).

Slurp down another beer, scratch groin unattractively, and belch.

Cover, and quickly fry until golden brown, turning at least once.

Drain excess oil on paper towels.

Serve with a jar of moonshine and a Marlborough cigarette with the filter removed.

Put on a *Shit Happens* or soiled *John Deere* hat.

 Discipline the spawn with a stout tree limb.

Keith Pepperell

5. Sir Quimbush Merkin's Calf Testicles in White Wine Sauce

Well-known Suffolk, England eccentric and champion professional croquet player the late Sir Quimbush Merkin OM, VC acquired this famous recipe from the then Dali Lama in the public bar of Ye Olde Black Pigge Pub just after the First World War. A keen darts player and vegetarian his Divinity was rather oddly fond of an occasional game of darts. Unknown to the DL, Quimbush Merkin had been World Champion in 1909 and 1911.

The DL rather unwisely bet on the best of five games an extremely rare testicle recipe from The Vatican library he had obtained from Pope Pius XI against a small bowl of rice.

It transpired the original recipe was an 1549 Papal Inquisition favorite used to combat Protestantism by substituting heretic's testicles for those of a calf.

Ingredients

1 cup cheap dry white wine (drink the rest swiftly)

1 cup water

40 locally sourced calf testicles

1 or 2 cloves of fresh garlic (roughly chopped)

Chopped white or yellow Onion to taste

2 Tablespoons corn starch,

Nun-blessed salt and ground white pepper and your favorite hot sauce to taste {seasonings - see *post*}

Method

Wash and clean the calf testicles thoroughly. Boil them until nice and tender, about 40 minutes or so should do nicely. Drink a couple of ball jars of Wild Turkey and/or flog a lazy manservant while you are waiting.

Drain your testicles thoroughly.

Sauté your testicles together with the onion and garlic until a nice golden brown. Don't burn them!

Dissolve the corn starch and water in a chipped old cup, then add to your testicles.

Add wine and let simmer until sauce thickens.

Finally, add your favorite seasonings and serve steaming hot.

Toast Sir Quimbush in an appropriate manner.

6. Lady Estima Davenport's Ortega Salsa Lamb Balls

If there had ever existed a modern-day monstrous regiment of women Lady Estima Davenport would, most certainly, have been its Colonel-in-Chief with her old school chum and tennis partner Muriel Dinwiddy as her able subaltern. Indeed immediately following the first blast of a Knoxian trumpet either lady would have instantly seized it and poked it ungraciously into the blowhard's bottom.

Both ladies were red hot socialists, despite their elevated stations in life. Lady Estima had, in 1924, clouted Winston Churchill with her handbag. Churchill was Chancellor of the Exchequer at the time under the happy simpleton Stanley Baldwin, whom Muriel despised with a passion. She had once quite vulgarly claimed at a woman's rally that he was "living proof that sodomy could produce children." her Ladyship was promptly arrested, thrown into a black maria, and later fined ten shillings at the Bow Street Magistrates Court. She paid her fine with four hundred and eighty farthings.

It had transpired Baldwin had enraged Lady Davenport when he had spoken of 'the impracticability of socialism.'

Muriel Dinwiddy had flown at Churchill during a rather posh dinner at the Mansion House calling him "a stumpy, boggle eyed piss artist". This confrontation occurred soon after Britain's disastrous return to the gold standard resulting in unemployment, deflation, and the miners' strike that precipitated the General Strike of 1926.

Some mashed potatoes had also been propelled in Winnie's general direction.

On another occasion, while in her cups, Muriel had bellowed to Winnie "call yourself a boozer, I could drink you under the table with both of my hands tied behind your back."

Winston, who much later in 1953, was to win The Nobel Prize for Literature, beating out among others Ernest Hemingway, retorted with a pretty accurate farting noise.

Both ladies were terribly fond of testicles and this recipe was presented to Lady Davenport by the celebrated French chef Henri – Jules Noixdeporc at Wimbledon after the valiant ladies had soundly thrashed the hirsute French pairing of Salomé and Capucine-Enola La Touche in straight sets 6-2 6-1 in the Championship Match.

Ingredients

1 quart lamb testicles(U.S. quart = approx. 1 litre)

1 large yellow onion chopped

 3 cloves garlic finely chopped

3 tablespoon fresh parsley with stalks removed 1 small can Ortega chilies.

1 (7 ounce) can Ortega salsa

¼ cup white wine (guzzle the rest quickly)

Nun-blessed salt and ground white pepper to taste.

Several bottles of Guinness for

drinking during preparation

Method

Cook the lamb testicles in boiling salted water for about 20 minutes making sure to remove the unattractive foam from the water as it appears. When cooked and tender, drain and rinse your testicles well in cold water.

Fry the onion and peppers in a little oil. When onion and peppers are wilted, add the chopped garlic and parsley. Add testicles and fry for a few minutes. Add the Ortega salsa, nun-blessed salt, ground white pepper, and white wine and simmer away covered for about 15 minutes.

Drink several gin and tonics and be surly to the help

7. Barb 'Tubby' Tollbooth - Change's Lamb Testicles in White Wine Sauce

Unattractively plump Barb Tollbooth-Change is a well-known and universally reviled Law Office Receptionist with the venal Mid-West ambulance chasers of Globocnik, Stangl, Blobel, Kaltenbrunner, Dirlwanger, Globocnik, and Mengele (Catch Phrase "We don't get laid if we don't get paid". Her unpleasant disposition ideally suits her for a career in the client service industry. Formerly an unsuccessful insurance agent and grocery store assistant manager fat Barb has the kind of rasping voice that might easily open a safe. She appears on local television as a compensated spokesperson for the firm's sickening commercial seeking to represent simpletons who might have been startled by insects on fruit.

 Her testicle recipe was acquired as part payment of a retainer by a client who suffered a closed neck injury while recoiling during an alleged aphid incident.

Ingredients

About 40 lamb testicles per person

2 cloves of crushed garlic

½ large yellow onion - finely chopped

2 tablespoons corn starch

1 cup cheap white wine (guzzle the rest)

Nun-blessed salt and ground white pepper
   to taste

A little Tabasco or favorite hot sauce
   to taste
   1 cup water

Method

Wash and clean your testicles thoroughly.

Boil until tender skimming away nasty looking scum as necessary for about 45 minutes.

Drain thoroughly.

Fry your testicles, yellow onion and garlic until brown (make sure not to burn).

Dissolve corn starch in warmish water; add to the testicles.

Add the white wine and let simmer gently until the sauce thickens nicely.

Continue to stir gently.

Add the seasonings to taste and serve nice and hot.

Drink several bottles of stolen wine

and start the 'creative billing process' to squeeze as much loot, swag, and lolly as possible from a feeble-minded client.

8. Goat Juggler Afasi Otinati's Famous Samoan Goat Gonad Stew

Plucky Samoan superstar and celebrated goat juggler, the massive Afasa Otinati is a triple heavyweight Champion at this former Navigator Islands' traditional sport. The fa'a Samoa or traditional Samoan way, remains a strong force in Samoan life,goat juggling, and politics. Despite centuries of European influence, Samoa maintains its historical customs, social and political systems, and language Cultural customs such as the Samoa 'ava goat juggling and goat gonad stew eating ceremony are significant and solemn rituals at important occasions including the bestowal of matai goat wrestling titles. Items of great cultural value include the finely stitched goat scrotum purse.

Ingredients

A nice big pair of goat testicles
Heavily salted water
1 nice big yellow onion
Several chili peppers
2 handfuls of chopped Celery
Enough potatoes for two servings
Cup of margarine
Some nice fresh, firm Brussels sprouts
(for two servings)
2 cups of Samoan chunked taro root

Method

Take your nice, well cleaned, big pair of goat testicles and boil away in a big pot of salted water

Add the onions roughly chopped
together with the taro root, chili
peppers, and celery.

Boil away for one and a half hours

Boil some potatoes in salted water and
then mash with some gonad stew juice
and margarine.

Mash the potatoes with some juice from
the stew, and a cup of margarine.

Fry some Brussels sprouts until nicely
caramelized.

Serve with two cases of beer.

9. Mrs. Fang 'Chop-Chop' Dong's Rooster Testicle Soup

Fang Dong, widow of the late, great
oriental restauranteur Sum Hung Dong,
continues to oversee The Sun of Heaven
Restaurant in Shanghai. Her two
identical twin elder sons Ding Dong
and Ju-Long Dong have carried on the

Dong tradition of culinary excellence.

Rooster testicles are a little bit like small sausages with an annoying 'tofu-like' texture. Oriental testicle buffs like them "barely cooked so they are very tender." "They have velly mild flavor", Mrs. Dong advises "they are a little like chicken rivers."

Chinese community markets frequently carry rooster testicles. Mrs. Dong's ancestors have been cooking and eating rooster testicles for over five thousand years, or so she claims.

Ingredients

12 ounces of rooster testicles

1 pint of chicken broth

Handful of freshly quartered Shitake mushrooms

Three finely chopped scallions, including green tops

Some whole canned baby sweetcorn

A few water chestnuts

A little sesame oil

A little chili oil

A pinch of ground white pepper to taste

A pinch of ground ginger

Method

Make a nice broth by combining all of the ingredients save the rooster testicles.

Clean the testicles and remove any 'dangling bits'.

Simmer the testicles in the broth for about fifteen minutes or so.

Serve with Chinese Rice Wine and a little boiled rice.

10. Mrs. Indira Patel's Kapura Bakra Masala (Curried Lamb Testicles)

Indira Patel (nee Patel) is the youngest daughter of corner newsagent mogul Vagapussi Patel and an award winning chef. She appeared on the popular television cooking show *Chopped* and became a chopped champion. Her pickled horse penis bought tears to the host's eyes.

Ingredients

1pound cleaned lamb testicles
¼ cup ghee:
2 cups yellow onions peeled and finely chopped
3 cloves Garlic peeled and crushed
1 square inch of ginger peeled and finely chopped

1 medium Serrano pepper with white
pith removed finely chopped: 2

¼ teaspoon turmeric powder:

2 teaspoons coriander powder

1 teaspoon cumin powder:

¼ teaspoon ground cayenne

¼ teaspoon black pepper ground:

¼ teaspoon salt:

2 Tablespoons water

Juice of half fresh lime

Method

Wash your lamb testicles.

Cut each testicle along the middle in
half.

Peel off the skin and discard it.

Cut each testicle in half length-wise
to result in two oval shaped slices

Soak sliced testicles in cold salted
water (4 cups of water with 2
Tablespoon of salt) for about one
hour.

Drain and wash in clean water. Pat dry
with paper towel.

Heat ghee in a frying pan

Add onions and gently fry till edges
turn a light brown.

Add garlic, ginger and Serrano. Stir.
Fry for about one minute

Add turmeric powder, coriander, cumin,
cayenne, black pepper, and salt and
fry for about one minute

Add sliced testicles. Stir and fry

till testicles have changed color.

Add water and stir vigorously.

Cook covered for about seven minutes
for desired consistency
Stir in the squeezed lime juice.
Enjoy with best Basmati rice.

Keith Pepperell

ABOUT THE AUTHOR

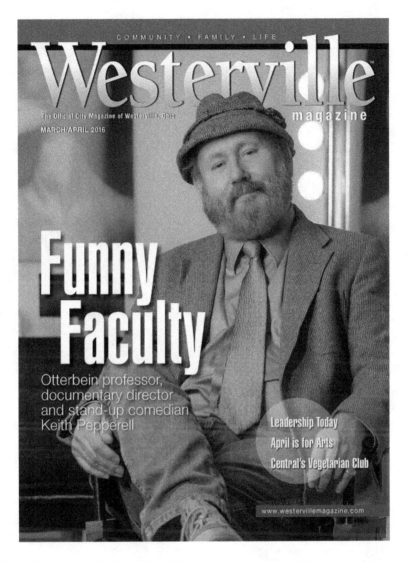

Little is known about the author since he entered a witness protection program. He has written eighty-six books and is likely as mad as a cut snake.

Printed in the USA
CPSIA information can be obtained
at www.ICGtesting.com
LVHW091646021123
762911LV00006B/106

9 781545 030301